VISITATION

VISITATION

POEMS

B. A. Libman

ORPHÉE
Orphée Press

Contents

Catabasis	2
California October	4
Via Negativa	6
This Life	8
Yeartime	9
Montréal October	10
What It's Like	11
Sweet Dreams	13
Virus	14
Nouvelle-France	15
Put Some Water On It	16
Sabbath Elegy	17
Autumn Elegy	19
Old Republican Calendar	21
Eli, Eli	23
language	24
Greens	25

91st & Broadway	26
YOU CALLING ME COLD-HEARTED?	28
A Supermarket in California, 2020	29
The Dreamer	31
Poem	32
The Unlovable Poet	33
Nothing Left to Eat	37
Afternoon Nap	39
Object-Oriented Ontology	40
Silhouette at the End of an Alley	43
False Memories of a Bygone Era	45
Saint Brendan of Hull, MA	46
The Tormented Novelist	48
Dans un sommeil que charmait ton image	49
Allegory for a Holiday	51
Visitation	52
The Food Network	54
Hephaestus, After	56
Phantom	57
The Lewy Body Problem	58
Glory, Glory	59
Sestina in the Dark	60
Anabasis	62

For J. H.

Copyright © 2021 by B. A. Libman

All rights reserved. No part of this book may be reproduced in any manner whatsoever without written permission except in the case of brief quotations embodied in critical articles and reviews.

First Printing, 2021

I went down to the Piraeus yesterday with Glaucon, son of Ariston...
　　　　—Plato

What, then, blinded me? My clearsightedness. What misled me? My straightforward spirit. What makes it happen that every time my grave opens, now, I rouse a thought there that is strong enough to bring me back to life? The very derisive laughter of my death.
　　　　—Blanchot

Catabasis

    You came, also,
    twining ivy, with
    the natural crowd
    to comfort
    the poet in his cold
    sorrows.

    More than looking back, more than outstretched
    arms which could not connect, more than three Suns without women,
        the solitude gripped you upon the shadeless hill, the pin grasses cut
        erect into your backside, and the world gathered itself there by the ash
        -tree, the holm-oak, the many-colored maple, the rosy-fingered
        excess, moose with molted antlers, birds of paradise, ears trained to
        contain the tree-line. You sang of boys mourned by the gods, the
        Cypress once a lithe lad pink and pursuing a silver stag, striking
        swiftly into the jugular, panting alongside him, dying alongside him
        to know what it feels like, his legs growing pale green, his ears
        hardening to bark-reef, his hair the spiral grain of wooden crown:
        he stood peering down the cliff-distance. You, poet, sang of girls
        possessed by forbidden fire, their flesh molten, greening
        with the object. The girls gathered round.

O, Orpheus, the land embraces you and will not turn
its head. "I will mourn for you: you will mourn
for others and
                descend
                        into sorrow."

California October

I came back to California for my things, the sky
particulate, the royal road blue with your absence.
I could die with remembering: one should never arrive

in an ancient place at night. I wash off the plane journey
in a lemon-bright bathroom, bone-tiled and stained with old
hair, the grime of wantonness. Right away I could die with wanting

to leave, to come back to you, caught in the distance
of a tired country. I spend empty days reading and not
taking care of the place, which is temporary and untaut.

A stray seagull has made it over the Santa Cruz mountains, far
from the shocking surf, and landed on my unspeaking balcony. He
waddles in flat carrot feet and tells me that I have lost, that I have held

   open too many doors at once to preserve my own stupid freedom.
   The mountain gale has pummeled them shut and I have returned here
   through a valve, to California, purgatory of America. It won't be

   long before I flex the ash-stiffened shocks of the tired car and tunnel
   the miles back to you. In my dreams we had never left

this place, or I had never left my things, or you

had never stopped thinking of me.

Via Negativa

On the mountain it is white and quiet except your breathing and knees
>> in the crackling snow.

Slit in the blue distance, the feta sheet has slipped quietly away, a bird,
>> then
>>>> a thundering
>>>>>> reaches you.

Now the little men file archaeologically down in a panic. No one knows
>> where to look.
>>>> It cannot be proven,
even with your high technology. They must search by way of negation,
>> their lithe purple-striped poles
>>>> retractable, unretracted, spearing
the crystal snow in spirals like ants drawn to Calypso. "No," they say.
>> "Not here," tightening.
>>>> Soon the unspeaking center grows swollen
with its nothing, and in the distance collapses into a space no larger
>> than an ant. The spiraling
>>>> stops,
the shovels sharpened and processed in a ritual of the understanding.

This Life

When I die please
let them know
that I lived
always
on time's
horizon, never
listening, never living
in the moment,
as they said,
nor letting
myself be,
and so to die
must not
have been
any big thing.

Yeartime

    I lie down on the lilies and grow nostalgic for my old age as one grows
                fond of lives never lived.
    You at 50 were so battered by the war with the insurance company
                over the failed table leg and the dent it put in your femur.
    You at 65 were so ugly and unwilling to lay down on the red sofa with
                the blue and yellow threaded checks.
    You at baby's height were so preoccupied with the shins of adults,
                the crumbs of dinner snacks, cocktail napkins,
    and had not yet decided what desire you would grow into and fail
               yourself by at seventeen.
    You, illuminated in the sepulcher, wonder whether it is all just a joke,
                like that time you saw your own daughter
    skipping by you when you were sixteen, and you asked her when
                the bus was leaving
    and she said, "You fool. You old fool."

Montréal October

even so the cars go on
the lady with the white scarf
pleads with her blue-chip dog
the general autumn falls through
the canopy bristling like one
caught in the prosaic cold

What It's Like

I miss you like
an old man misses the red-faced lad who cut his grass for years
before his wife died, and for years after her going, and who called him
pops and drank beers with him from a cooler between the lawn chairs,
with evening swimming on and the milky drippings of stars and the
warm asthmatic silence. The pair would talk in sighs, desiring or
letting go, the chairs bearing them into the growing anonymity.

"That must be Gawd," the lad would say, and the old man
would get weepy in the blue dark, wiggling his toes inside
the worn loafers. He missed the lad already, young and slipping
through the years, the paper route and the twine-pulled teeth
behind him, maybe some college soon, a pebble's toss in that long
hallway he was nearer the beginning than the end of. The man wept
unspeaking, smiling, the beer sweet like apricot softening, sticking to
his lips. He missed that lad for his becoming, missed him like a satellite
in its mad orbit. He stares mottled through the yellow water of his eyes
and would to Gawd that he could keep the motes of years
from clinging to his shoulders.

Sweet Dreams

I cannot breathe for
a mouthful
The SS-Hauptsturmführer
Laughs and laughs
He draws and pulls
In haughs, in haughs
I scrape, you scrape
We scrape, he clasps
He cranks and leaks
The gas, the gas

Virus

You called me a reaper
of lost desire, and since
then I have wandered
empty along the oil-softened
passageways, listening to the cants
of transients, weeping for a time
before my affliction.

Like Poseidon my skin is older
than the sea, cultivating loss
like a fungus: it was you who
smuggled
the spores into my armpits.

With the last dime
deposited, I leave the sorry
motel rooms, taking the holes
in the bedsheets with me.

Nouvelle-France

Where do you go, Bretons, Acadians?
Wither shall I follow you tonight with your green-lit
shops and your two dollar chocolate bars and your men and women
in greasy love on the benches of the blue park? How many times
have I sought you in this place, where the pond outstrips all of its
trappings and the ducks moan for some greater delight? Where
else would you be if not for the virtuous sketching of two gentlemen
wrapped in glory and visions of a land bestraddled by a river?

The young couples pass and throw out their signs
to the nearest trashcan. The old woman who rummages
there is looking for some Crystal to help her proceed
with her general wanderings along this harrowed hill within a wider
body. How shall I address you, O French province, sitting proudly
atop slaughtered land, drinking long from a blood not yours, feeling
the slit in your side from the English knife? You will not stop
your moaning until the baby is removed. But what do I know, old
transplanted Jew, not one for divination or mailbox lotteries.
I cannot understand you when you are like this, but we could not be
together if it were any other way, for I am unable to live among you,
O different Canadians, without some assurance
that you won't spread your watery legs for another.

Put Some Water On It

The ash from upstate
has caressed my window—
glass fire, they call it. Shrieking:
a child: bare feet slapping
the concrete that zags orthogonally
through the complex. I am sweating
in my undershirt, and down there
the lace shadow is spare. Someone will hang
its spackle on the clothesline.

It is somebody's birthday. Mariachi
music reaches the window with
the parade of plates, triptych tacos
from the truck across the street.
Autumn—
How different you are in your infirmity!
Tender you tongue the edges of days and hope
the saliva travels along the fibers. On the 280
with the light going I wave to you, as you haul your
sack of mists over the Santa Cruz mountains, bearing
the gift of sea-salted air for all. A little lands on my lips.
"Hola señor," the birthday girl says, sighting me
in the smoke-flecked window. I smile: if I am
dead I should not be stirred.

Sabbath Elegy

I'm going away for a while.
I promise not to hand you
over, nor your crazy running

spirit. Just yesterday I saw
you bending a booklet trying to hear
the sense. Or when you cried with broken

knees: that was difficult. I have seen the men
gathered at the shore, tense, gripping, sun-blazoned,
eyeing the horizon for the fishbone mast. Shirtless they stare

down the leaving, like a spacecraft meant
for nobody, evaporating thickly into the vacuum-
less future. It'll just be a little while, like the origin

of the universe. And one day, stirring
your tea, you will hear the chime of my leaving,
the knock in the floorboards of your sorrow.

I have seen your face with its tide
all pulled out. I will not give you away, you
with your stirring, and me, full of time, inhaling

what remains of the expansion.

Autumn Elegy

For Jesse Galganov, 1995-2017

Every autumn I have watched the space between
objects with your name on it, small diluvian dreams
you'll return with the sweet year

The first artist was Cain for the first
sin was duplication—we plunder
from mounds to mound other bodies

Your mother makes posts and bruises the air
screaming, the golden poppy grows
like a weed here and still you never picked it

You've not been lain while the ice holds you
or the mulch or the goat dung or the riverbed.
Only one was ever buried twice

You lift coins of ice to your lips
when you cross, the boat in perigee, the lattice
flows and the acrid staff plumbs the silt

I have dreamed of a poppy blue and purulent,
that from Peru each thing sucks its tail

and from the trail you've seen the end already

I have dreamed that on a train the track
ticks with the rain that runs through
the canvas roof—the car is empty save you,

And your hair uncurls and drains its ink into the glacier
where you dissolved and each word sinks
the question with the water. You only kiss

your finger and shake your head / i need you
You cannot cross back to where you disappeared
where you've lived inside me every year

I have dreamed that your sister cries
on one-lane roads and bloodies her fingers
on the asphalt looking for you

When the day before you left I told you
what to read that I loved you, not to die
what was funny was the irony

In my dreams you grow old you give me
golden poppies you swim in trains that tick
as mountains go you row on row on row on row

Old Republican Calendar

I blow over the coals,
the spirit on the waters, trying
to give you presence, where before I
was met only with now, here where you
had been.

Having been there before I know how
to find you, following the low walls to the bay
ing river, swollen and putrid with the feathered milk
of cigarette cartons, lamps arraying where they would hang
a martyred poet.

More than touch, taste—an atmospherics:
the way shadows vied for voices in the rheumatoid alley,
the way you hid humid in bistros, counting
the thirty bounties of Thermador, melon, ryegrass, horsetail,
mugwort, mullein, rapeseed, caper, lupin,
the way young countries made politicians of poets,
the way old ones made pundits of statesmen,
the way you walked always in relation, me behind, the sad streets
and yawning cats thrown out, nodes of a lonely Zodiac.

If I hold these things together in the hyperbole
of a glancing breath, I can keep you

alive, the way a thumb ignites figures in a flip book,
the reel stretched and tanned before the objective
light.

But I am unseen by whatever
has gone before, already a phantom,
and me, arranging the domestication
of embers to prove your having been
there.

Eli, Eli

Hannah Szenes, 1921-1944
From the Hebrew

My God, My God, that these shall not end on the Earth
The sand & the sea
The rustle of the waters
The storming of the heavens
The prayer of man

language

It wasn't so much chatter, talk of loss
        in translation
so much as a crooked belief in the skin
        of things. You
with your contempt for capitalization, flaying the twig
        of your language to reach
the point, bare-knuckling the verbiage that might bring this airship
        flaming into soft earth,
word and world come one against the other, the glove dissolving
        into the palm-lines, the shaking
hand. But you are munching the chaff to prove the falseness
of the wheat. Spare me your comma-
        less ambiguities.
There is no inside-text, just as the pith of the orange
        rides the skin.

Greens

Forest, lime, emerald, army, hunter, jade, mint, baby vomit, barium, beer bottles, pine needles, envy, resolve, the San Felipe hills after rainfall, the shallow waters of the calanques, golf balls at a ramshackle mini-putt, long leaves of Eucalyptus, broad ones of Oak, slimes, goops, venoms, safety vests, the correct answer, perfect avocado, permission, unripe banana, tyros, tongue after a lollipop, American money, mints at a steakhouse, half of all Christmases, grass of Parc Mont-Royal, lacklight at Lac Ouareau, grass of Kindersley park, long moss at Castle Rock, school uniforms, sea-glass trapped in the piles of the pier in Hull, MA, water at the pier in Hull, MA, stains on the shorts I used to own, *penecillium roqueforti*, alligator jaws, smoker's gums, the wart on a witch, a curse with a catch, alliteration, lake water, roasted beans, Ireland of my dreams, Ireland of Ireland, bitter herbs, men named Herb, women named Kelsey, Brazil from above, the trick light of a sunset, the first long thaw, brooding pus, skirts of all mountains, stems of alpine flowers, evolution, excess, old copper, older bogs, honest bedfellows. Beginnings,

91st & Broadway

I lay down—
phone, recharge.
long for sleep
for the silk to
drape the pregnant
bellies, the eyes
sliding tenderly across my chest
like mother's hand when
child has a cold

I wake
phone, charge
lips like pie crust flake
a yellow sun on a yellow day
the yellow cabs buzz, buzz

when I wake
squint at the sun and
my retinas ache
copper on my eyes
a dream within a wake

eyes burn and fade
while the day is made

up
of little nights
night, of little days

then descend, stay
glacial vacuum
cold and crystal on
window glass—

but strange there is no air
only dark this far
from the surface
repair a thousand years
trapped beneath
oyster's mark
tongue, a pearl

then night rides the day
With fluttering
lashes flight
and down, and phone
and recharge

YOU CALLING ME COLD-HEARTED?

You'll be hearing from my angina

A Supermarket in California, 2020

What am I to do with you, O guileless one? If they grew tired
of your schtick, it was because you were too much a Jew,
or too little. Strange buckle-bearded Walt Whitman, nasal
and unafraid to sing, they forgot how you carried us all

upon your queer shoulders, as you hid among the carrots and
the butter lettuce. You were meant to be with me, or I with
you, but the wonder of this place has vanished, the linoleum
scuffed and thickened with the contents of a half-century's broken

jams. Which way does your enchantment lead you tonight? They
have seen you riding your tireless bicycle under the moonlight,
just the rims finessing the glassy roads. But what they say is wrong:
sounds like Heaven. I've wandered the Bowery and the Lower
Haight for you, seeking your latest incarnation. You can only

have traded up,

rebirthing-wise, and so perhaps more Jewish than
before. You must be younger than me, Allen Ginsberg!
If only by two or three years. At the High Holidays I watch
for thick-haired men and women—that's how you'll be,

you who have had enough pate for many lifetimes. They
have forgotten the rightful heir to William Carlos Williams.
There is no more promise in America, no hidden seed for you
to pluck, O dialectical poet. The maid was an anti-Semite,

you were right. They do not know how right you were. It was
true, your vision of Blake: the hand of God was the sky, and also
the blue, and not their maker. Butler had no balls, old beatnik.
And America has no balls, either.

The Dreamer

the hilltop is green because you colored it that way
in the shadow of a window I watched the half
of your slim profile as you filed

the daily doings and became skeptical of your habits
but what do I know, estranged as I am from the way one picks

pebbles on the beach only to throw them at the birds
but they are only there if I say so, and when I say so it is less

clear and definite than when you have command, even as your hills
are green, your skies the color of skin, your humans loving and tender
and not disappointing

one another. The silences accrue and will be dusted
and dumped to make way for better imaginings.

Poem

And you pithy salesman
What will you have left but your vanity?
Whose cock will be washed and given
For the close? How many of you I have slept with,
how constant your chatter. And then how beautiful
you are, the only ones who can sing
the Wandrers Nachtlied, ballerinas of the green night. O night!
I wish it were the first time, when you saved me
and I did not yet know your ship.

The Unlovable Poet

I

We search for freedom, you and I, in these words
Here's a glass to magnify the third to last page you turned
Just there, in back
But anyway, the moment's past

What I'd like to say is there already
We read it, we two, together—remember?
Bring your finger here, steady,
See Kit Marlowe, just above:
'Come away with me, and be my love'
Freedom comes, then, when it must prove
It annihilates, like the evening bruise
In the sky; see, here's another:
'Let us go then, you and I'
And we shall the many pleasures
Something or other, forever

My eyes like weary legs have had enough.
This book, obtuse from wanton use
Let's close it, clap it shut
Make plumes of dust fly and glitter the air
Guide a dry palm through your greasy hair

And look—there, freedom shall away
Through a door shadow; will we follow
In a prance over scuffed parquet?
I'm callow but I've no more faith in reading
Today, tonight we should sharpen skates
Fly like poor wights into
Widest moon country

II

You'll know you love me
By the knuckle-rattle of your tightened fist
Gripping a wrist and thinking this
Is what arthritis is, the chatter of knees
In buckle, the subtle wisp of air as that bloody
Wraith goes by—see, just there, moody
And debonair

A shift in the small of your spinal
Column is all it takes to glimpse
The final footfall of that grinning sprinter
And smell, trembling, honeysuckle
In the moribund Berlin winter

And if you love me, on numb tiptoe
We'll skate in chase of skittish ghosts
Who hate silence and therefore know
In muffled Yiddish what freedom is
Who makes it most

III

I cool my feet against the snow

I beat my wings against the snow
Useless flaps, for decades now
These feathers here, they're just for show

Whether we go then, or not
We must move before my feathers rot

I swear to you, my dear, I care
Not, whether you turn heel there
See—on that spot, and set blaze
To the weeds and solstice trees and square
A weal on my tender thoughts; I paraphrase
Lord Alfred said it fair: better to have loved and lost
Than stood frostbitten, edgeways
With icicles chewing my hair

These old cobblestone roads
These oiled salmon skin roads
The acrid steam that fills my nose
All is glazed crystal, wax
Jacket winter air hibernating
In dreariest heart-thumps
Waiting for you or your
Foot's reply, just there

Silence now—there goes
Our ghost, evaporated
Wren. Your eyes follow our boot-prints
Shall we retire home, shall I quote
More poetic men? Or will you thieve me
Forward into dark, scrawl with pen
My flesh into witch-dance, each foot
Twisted—

You leave me and that
Was always an option and
I dig and dig to find the
Copse that snagged the sleeve of my pants

Nothing Left to Eat

I let drop
the bouillon
cube, watch
it break and
bellow, like a
rogue galaxy
making a
glamorous
run for it.
The broth
is murky and
the chicken
has come
a little way
to life. What
would that
be like? To
dissolve with-
out losing
myself, to
change state,
let slide my face
and edges. To be
everywhere and

nowhere, held
by whatever
container I found
myself in.

Afternoon Nap

Whatever we said on the red fabric couch
with the yellow blue threaded checks, whatever it was that plunged
usso deeply into Haydn or Brahms and whatever the dishwasher
triedto urge with its gurgling and the green night
reaching and yawning and wanting always to go to bed

how I wish I was that child that once I was
granted life service in a desert with a boat but no island
                          and a coconut
for a briefcase in which I kept my golden edged razor blades,
and howoften I thought that the two of us on the red couch
could dream this together

then on top of you looking deep into where I thought
you would be, the dream is split, and I see only myself in the well
where I drew the water to fill my coconut shells, and my brain
laid flat with a meat hammer and hung on the wire beneath the sun
and made never to think a thought that wasn't about sand or
loneliness or the first time I heard a dry music like certain wines

Object-Oriented Ontology

Peer through the hole of your world
Trace it with
Your finger and tear it
Gently wider
See?

He looks quite like you, is not
Feet from you,
A bespectacled man with long brown hair
Smoking rig after rig on the steps of
Philosophy Hall,
While the woman before him
Tall with blonde bob
Scratches an itch
On the back of her knee

You look down as your long
Brown hair obscures your right lens
And your left tennis shoe, which rests
On the bottom step of
Philosophy Hall

Before you she wrenches
Over awkwardly like an

Injured flamingo in a torrid pond
Her bob shifting ever so slightly
Forward
She reaches her right wing
Toward you
And with the other scratches the back of
Her knee through her jeans

In orbit along your periphery is
A twenty-something man,
Jeans, army-coloured backpack and Vans
From down the walkway along
The outer edge of the quad in front of
Philosophy Hall

You caught him
Before turning to
Find the spot behind
Your knee

He watches you the way
A sailor strains to precipitate the image
Formed by the difference of the porthole
And the droplets that cling to it
His observation bothers you and
You wonder what he sees

Nothing has felt so good as
Scratching that itch, but something
Is unfulfilled, blocked by a thin
Coarse barrier of denim
Like tying knots with mittens on

You look up toward your arm

Inadvertently pointed toward the young
Man
Whose brown hair droops down before
His nose and
You wonder if he needs
His spectacles
As he smokes a long rig on
the steps of Philosophy Hall

Silhouette at the End of an Alley

And wouldn't it have been alright to glide
        along the edge like
that? Wouldn't it have been
sound to keep your foot
        extended toward my lap,
to read down through
            the evening without getting
to the center of it all.
        What it is like is falling
            all the time,
                therefore orbiting.

In prisms the effect
        is interesting enough;
so too in the shadows I see
in our lighted doorway
        from down there
            in the street,
when I've come home
        from a long walk to clear
the hollowness
in my head, and have not yet decided

    whether I'll come
        in, this time round.

False Memories of a Bygone Era

And is that what you wanted? It wouldn't have been the trees,
        though sometimes I thought of them
while listening to the music that your mother made when she cooked
        ragù in her skirt and apron
with yellow feet cracked against the tile and baby you
        so small and delicate with your spilled
mouth, the very same which I kiss, but not before making you
        something delicious. I stretch out my hand and feel
for where you have been and I find you there. Isn't it funny?
        The hand thinks
better than the brain, like the other shoe before it

Saint Brendan of Hull, MA

> *Let pry through the portage of the head*
> *Like the brass cannon; let the brow o'erwhelm it*
> *As fearfully as doth a galled rock*
> *O'erhang and jutty his confounded base,*
> *Swill'd with the wild and wasteful ocean.*
> (Henry V, 3.1)

Beneath the pier at Pemberton the brine gasps,
pulled from the pebbles. On a mist-thickened
night the lobster cages linger in congregation.
They are destitute, having come a long way through
what is called the Gut. The husk of a man gathers
there, dwelling loosely among the rocks, his arms
roped with slime-slicked seaweed, the rest of him
tucked away in the barnacled exoskeletons of crabs
and the beards of mussels in cluster. He is a hero.
And with the sun-tide he will grow from concentrate
into the swift seeker of the shallows, the foul-smelling
angel of the pier, retrieving lost dollars and errant
oysters that evanesce through the boardwalk. He'll keep
the oysters, thank you very much, to shore up
his knee caps. You don't mind, do you? The rest

he returns in cobbled cairns up the beach before
his daily disassembly. He won't howl if you step on him,
or if you use lengths of his arms for your garden.
He likes that very much: to be of help to humans,
not quite one himself.

The Tormented Novelist

Try not to say anything obvious
    They hate that more than anything
        Better to watch the window sill and say
            something shocking (anything will do, comrade)
                Bear in mind that nothing grows that cannot

laugh at itself, as the Earth will whip the Earth reliably in thunder
In the street, a child chases his red ball: a thing is never so grave as
when it is funny

Dans un sommeil que charmait ton image

J'étais seul dans
mes rêves, derrière les
verres verrouillés

Lèvres doux, deux
pierres pareilles me
murmuraient avec

Le désert qui les
a lissés: Que veux-
tu, gueule blessée?

« Savoir où je me
suis porté mes pas
et à qui je m'adresse »

Mes prières. Les pierres
se sont posées comme
des poissons pétrifiés,

La pêche en sécheresse:
Nous ne savons pas, et

ne le saurons jamais.

Allegory for a Holiday

I am alive today! I called the writing
work, so that I might excuse myself
for a cigarette and something greasy and a hand
in someone's crotch. I am alive! and so are you, am so
because of you, and this way I dance enrobed by the red, blue,
tessellated tablecloth stitched and thickened like some dress
worn by an old peasant woman in a photograph of a memory
of the 19th century. You wonder what I do for society,
but isn't it enough to breathe life into you, to gather your breath
back into myself? Whoever thought one should have a ticket
to see the Uffizi sculptures was cooked from the start.
Today a friend and I painted the disgruntled head
of a lusterless bald man and ran laughing, spinning arcs
of lead-based carelessness into the air as one who knows
precisely what work is. So, are you here or not? Are you reading
this or not? And if not, then what are you? Go home to your dog
and steam your broccoli and wonder not
about the many trains you have missed
in the many midnights.

Visitation

Beyond the point of my foot, the long wooden
desk, uneven piles of books and the green chair
upholstered in sighing velvet. I almost expect
you to swivel there with that demonic smile, the way

you hated inhabiting abstractions, moved always
to the demotic, wickedly willing me along. I loved it—
I will you to swivel, but it is just a gust of air, in that chair,
or a phantom, not yours, separated from the crowd by

simplemindedness that led him to the sliding door
of my balcony. With flung wrist I offer an ostentatious
shirt to the whorling air. There, there, Gilded Ghost, take
shape and sign to me your story—but the golden garment

equips only the floor, prostrate, riveted like a dune. Did
you not even send an emissary? My mind emigrates to you
like the helicopter which could not find you in the dense
national park, where you complained of headaches and nausea

and asked the trees kindly which way was down. All ways, my son.
Hovering: that is all. You never swiveled in that chair, never
visited me in California. All that came after, and you don't know

how I've carried you here in pockets and cupholders and the other
slot
in the toaster. Won't you thaw in that glacier, or must the climate
do it

for you? Where have I seen you? I must cross the street and enter
the house of my past, where every room I am told is a memory. But
the gossamer contents—you are ever only in movement, slicking
time
along the hollow of your shoulder. Everywhere your face is gone, as
if

no matter how still you were I was always shooting you in transit.
I have only your copy, the space of the space where you had been.
They play tricks on my recollection: Is this our old room?
All the furniture has been
                                                            rearranged.

The Food Network

When I see a certain Brancusi I feel this kind of desire, that I want
            to hold it, more, to encompass it, squash its smooth curve into oblivion
                        somehow within me. This is why we watch those shows compulsively. Or it is the way
                        we watch them: always for the money shot, the dish entire, as it steams and sweats just after
                                    leaving the cook's hands and before it is delivered into the pink-yellow cavity of mouths. It is an aesthetic
                        object that is also a food object, its two modes converging in that perfect instant, and then, too,
                    in the second most important instant in a show like that, the reaction performed, etched
                into the face of the host after solemn first-bite. It is a whole sign-system
    communicating the fulfillment of that particular desire to us vicariously,
            or as vicariously as possible, for we never really stand-in. And rightly: not
                    being able to stand in is what enables us to keep watching: desire always seeks its own
                                extinction, and once you've extinguished it by mouth or member, it vanishes (for a time). My pleasure

at watching a food show is vastly diminished if I've just eaten a meal. Isn't that odd? It is art that inhibits the extinction of desire, in its own way, by its cool resistance, its colloidal unassimilability, because one cannot consume a Brancusi or the Grand Canyon for that matter. If the intellect and a certain more complicated space of emotions have a role in helping us feel and enjoy beautiful things, they do it alongside and on top of fundamental desire.

And because desire has direction,
        beauty is placed always at the end of its arrow,
hardened everlasting to the hunger.

When I look at a sublime mountain-face and see,
faintly, the chalk-white imprint of switchbacks,
rising like smoke from the valley to the peak —
I see   ——   desire.

Hephaestus, After

To life, Fire Child! From clay and iron ore.
The day is done, the tools in disarray:
I lay my shambles darkly at the shore.

The god himself stood proudly at my door,
His thick calves cut, his ringlets gold and gray,
To life, Fire Child! From clay and iron ore.

In shadow veiled, the child's guarantor,
Athena, watched, and begged my hand to stay.
I lay my shambles darkly at the shore.

"If not for this," she said, drawing ichor
From her vein, "we would not this girl mislay."
To life, Fire Child! From clay and iron ore.

My sorrow fell and touched the ocean floor,
"You, too, Ergane, know I must obey!"
I lay my shambles darkly at the shore.

"Take her to the quay; catapult her o'er."
In shrieking gale, we dragged her to the bay.
To life, Fire Child! From clay and iron ore.
I lay my shambles darkly at the shore.

Phantom

John Brown's body lies
moldering in my mind. Slick jaw, ice
in the eyes, raven hair—something
of Beckett in him.

Mine eyes hath seen the glory of the coming,
I say to you, and we watch naked from the fire
escape as pickpockets gather like soldiers
in the alley to assess their booty. "I would rather not
think of the past." Well it would rather not think
of you. "What else should motivate a ghost?" Nothing.
The army of the Lord hath been
disbanded. "Yet he's there, sifting buttons
from change." John Brown wants nothing
from you or from
this life,
only passage
home.

The Lewy Body Problem

He reaches for the buttermilk and wants to tell you about that thing

which he spent his life becoming an expert on

when I was

someone wipes the spittle

that thing which

that when I was

that thing

a crooked finger touches the pulsing temple, where he summits a memory

that which I

was

Glory, Glory

Lambent lies
the lithograph
of the lilting
lilies, gleaming,
glittering lee
along the glacier,
glowing
in the gloaming
of the lade:
glamorous light!

Sestina in the Dark

I killed a phosphorescent man today
It was easy in the dark,
Where the edge of form is lost
And the self-expansion blooms.
He did not even mind to die,
Untie his bifurcated soul.

He was a quiet skeptic of the soul
Just as he doubted today.
"Life casts you on a single die,"
He said, amalgamating dark.
"Without photosynthesis blooms
A black flower of freedom lost

On the forest floor, where once I was lost."
He dug two graves: for him and his soul.
"One is where the other blooms,"
He said, for the last time, today.
His lips were coral, his eyes dark,
He pinched a flea to see it die.

"I must see death again before I die.
The Nothingness I seek is lost
In confusing death with dark:

Neither shade nor light nor soul
Admits a funeral today.
The black behind the black: it blooms."

Along his pink neck the desert blooms,
Black barnacles about to die.
I thanked him for the trip today
And felt the weight of all I'd lost
And saw inside one grave, my soul
And in the other all was dark.

He said: "The body is a work of dark,"
Or was it I? The notion blooms,
Precipitate of tired soul.
We joined our bodies then to die,
To seek the loss behind what's lost.
Was I the man I killed today?

Beyond the dark, another time to die
Blooms steady like grief in I, who have lost
An only ragged soul, his sole today.

Anabasis

Deep beneath the mantle lies a half-hollow cavern, domed tortoise,
        cache to a profound and purple lake.
Murky-skinned decapods, green-eyed and crimped, live there
depositing crystalline
        spheres of human memory
onto the gleaming silver coral. They float blinkered by the billions,
unseeing of one another, but their vision
        is deep. They have glimpsed all
that you have forsworn, neglected, frightened yourself by with
forgetting. They feed on your life-storage, digesting
        the garbled
moments into translucent globes of time, pearls that populate the
deep tortoise belly. This is precisely where death
        struggles, its bunny-
hill, its kiddie pool. Faced with mere life it gnaws like a kitten
on a pigeon bone. The slightest cell
        excels, even here,
suffocated among the tortoise organs. Death has never been more
pathetic, tearing down a monument with strands
        of your hair.

B. A. Libman is a novelist, poet, and critic from Montreal, Canada. His work has been published in several literary magazines and reviews. He lives in California.

www.ingramcontent.com/pod-product-compliance
Lightning Source LLC
Chambersburg PA
CBHW020914080526
44589CB00011B/596